I0782643

WHAT ARE YOU WAITING for?

Develop Your Personal Style and Make More Money!

Darren Chilton

Table of Contents

Told with humor, and packed with tips and lessons from more than 25 years in the service industry, Darren Chilton cites real-life examples in this impactful and often hilarious look at finding your own service style - and giving yourself a pay raise.

This book is for any person who is currently waiting tables or is contemplating a position in the restaurant or hospitality industry, and wants to find a personalized style to enhance their abilities, and subsequently increase tips.

By the end of the book, readers will have a good understanding of their own individual style and how to apply those attributes into better service and greater income.

This book is an excellent resource for servers, hosts, managers, owners, or anyone in a face-to-face customer service related profession with a desire to dramatically improve service and guest retention.

INTRODUCTION

True, genuine service seems to be a lost and forgotten art form. When you experience it, it can bring a smile to your face and make you a customer for life.

That one moment, when someone extends real kindness and projects a desire to serve, can be priceless. For a server, it can mean more money in your pocket, regular guests who specifically request you, and guests who will frequent your establishment because you work there.

Picture this. It's a typical Friday night. A roomful of hungry, impatient guests wait to be served. The line of patrons waiting to get in extends out the door. The foyer is swamped with red-faced people demanding the tables they were promised 20 minutes ago.

You skip through the dining room, undaunted, announcing, "Hot...right behind you!" as you calmly and confidently glide to your table with a warm and genuine smile. You handle several tables at once, commanding anywhere from 20% and higher in tips at each table, and are often requested by returning guests. Because of your knowledge of the menu, you routinely increase your check averages by suggesting food and beverage pairings that enhance your guests' experiences.

In a nutshell, you are a badass! Like the famous sword fight scene in *A Princess Bride* when Cary Elwes responds to Mandy Patinkin who remarks, "You are *wonderful!*," and Elwes says, "Thank you. I have worked hard to become so."

You, too, must work hard to become that super server. Then, with cat-like reflexes, you will be able to negotiate the rocky terrain that is the dining room, and conquer it with your trusty sword. (Ok, that might be a bit much, but you get what I'm slinging.)

Thought...in today's world of nearly zero customer service, it is easy to separate yourself from the pack. The difference will be tangible.

So, what are you *Waiting* for?

BE YOURSELF

If being nice, gracious and accommodating to people is something you don't enjoy, you likely should find another profession. If it is not in you, faking it will be noticeable. Are you the type of person who is openly friendly, says "Hello" to strangers, gives way to others? If so, it is likely you would make a great server.

It is obvious which servers are in this business solely for the money and which servers enjoy serving people. If you are in this business to serve, you will make money. If you are in this business to make money, you had better learn how to be your best self in front of those who will be paying your salary (the guests).Being genuine is being real. But to be clear, being yourself doesn't necessarily mean throwing caution to the wind and showing your radical or rebellious side. That approach likely won't serve you well in the service industry.

Being your best self has more to do with personality and style than appearance. But your physical self does play a big role, too. Remember, you are serving food and beverages from your hands. Your face and mouth will be within a foot of your guest's meal, so it is vital to look and smell your best.

Most, if not all restaurants, hotels, etc., have a specific dress code. Unless you are working for an extremely progressive concept (which is certainly popular and a growing industry), it is likely you will need to follow certain rules regarding dress code. Being *you* sometimes means choosing the type of place that will welcome your individualism and style. Fine dining is not the only way to make money as a server. If you find a place that suits your style, you will make money.

I used to work for a restaurant called Bobby McGee's. Now an outdated concept, McGee's was one of the first of its kind. Its blueprint was to provide good food in an atmosphere of fun, often accompanied by a touch of irreverence. They carved out a unique niche by costuming the staff as characters such as Zorro, Robin Hood, Al Catraz, Buffalo Chips (the cowboy) and many, many more. I played the part of Rocky Balboa, and I had the time of my life.

This kind of concept is not for everyone. With a repertoire of nearly 75 birthday and anniversary songs, you had to be able to carry a tune and certainly couldn't be timid. McGee's attracted outgoing servers, many with backgrounds in music and theater. Our salad bar was an enormous bathtub filled with everything you could want. Often when guests would go to the salad bar, we would hide their table from them. We'd thrill at the looks on guests' faces when they went back to their seats to discover their table missing!

As 'Rocky,' the guests expected me to be a little punchy, so I was able to get away with behaviors I would never carry out in a 'normal' restaurant. For example, we greeted each table with a round of waters served with a lemon wheel. When a guest asked if they could get water without lemon, I immediately reached in with my finger, grabbed the lemon and slung it to the floor. The guests loved it!

15% Tip: Find a restaurant (hotel, etc.) that appeals to your personal style and dine there. You will quickly know if it seems like a good fit.

20% Tip: Be your *best* self. A truly passionate server is a successful one.

30% Tip: Reach outside your comfort zone to find a restaurant that will challenge you. For example, if you want to work in fine dining, and don't have wine experience, go get it. Learn as much as you can. Take classes. Practice on your friends and family. The resources are available if you really want it.

What's *your* style?

HOW TO ENGAGE

Perhaps the greatest way to engage with a guest is to have fun. It seems simple, but when you are enjoying yourself, you smile, your pace is quick, and you are in command. The easiest way to have fun is to know everything you need to know. When you have perfected memorizing the menu and fully understand and can execute the sequence of service, your confidence will soar through the roof. With confidence comes the ability to relax and enjoy what you are doing. This positive attitude will be obvious to the guest.

Develop the ability to really listen. When a guest is asking a question or looking for a recommendation, they should feel like they are the only one in the room. Many servers are distracted by other tables in their section when guests are trying to talk to them. Eye contact is vital with the guest you are speaking with.

I was in a Subway recently and the sandwich maker asked me all the important questions about what I would like on my sandwich. With each question, she would look directly over my head, avoiding eye contact. Have you ever experienced something like this? Her intent to avoid my gaze was so apparent that the couple behind me in line would snicker every time I looked above my head to see what she was looking at.

If you are new to this industry and need some practice, try setting up a mock-scenario at your home. Invite friends and family over to rehearse your introduction. This is an excellent way to get comfortable in front of others and practice your delivery, verbiage, body language and posture.

When I was an acting coach, I required my students to rehearse their lines in front of their mirror at home, by themselves. This can be extremely uncomfortable at first, but well worth the initial embarrassment. As a server, your main 'speech' at your respective tables will come at the beginning, during the introduction. This is where you establish your style in front of the guests and set the tone for the remainder of the service cycle.

Engaging the guest is all about making each individual feel important, seen, heard and understood. One of the greatest advantages you have is that they are already where they are, with the expectation and desire to be served, to eat and to drink. They are expecting you and realize that they will be listening to you. In other words, you have the floor.

15% Tip: The very least you need to do is smile. A warm and real smile will go a long way in the eyes of the guest.

20% Tip: Eye contact is of vital importance. Guests must know that you are genuinely interested in, and acknowledging, what they are saying.

30% Tip: The way you carry yourself speaks volumes. It will tell if you are confident or timid. Guests are most impressed with confidence (but never arrogance) when it comes to being served. In the words of former football coach, Bill Parcels, "Confidence is borne of demonstrated ability." The more you do it, the better you become.

What's *your* style?

APPEARANCE AND HYGIENE

The most basic rule of all: If you stink, you shouldn't be delivering food. If your nails and hands are dirty, you shouldn't be serving anything.

Most restaurants and hotels have specific and often strict dress codes for employees. If you find it too conservative, or too progressive, you may not fit in.

The guests we serve are naturally - and rightfully - particular when it comes to food handling and cleanliness. The more aware you are of this, the better for your wallet. It is extremely obvious when a server has not taken proper care of the hands, nails, breath, body odor, even shoe smell! Ah, there's nothing more appetizing than a refreshing burst of dirty sock air as the server plants his nasty shoes near you and your date.

Make sure your entire uniform is clean. All too often, servers approach with a filthy apron, not realizing that for seated guests, the apron is front and center in their path of vision.

Your place of employment will also have extremely strict hand washing guidelines. Follow them. If hand washing is not a priority where you work, make it one! It's not only about appearance, but more importantly, health and hygiene, for everyone and everything you're in contact with.

I worked at a fairly high-end establishment in the Cherry Creek Mall near Denver. The uniform included a white, cotton, buttoned-down long sleeve shirt, black pants and black bistro apron. All items were required to be ironed and starched. When it became obvious that the servers with the crispest uniforms were the ones making the most money, an unspoken contest emerged in which servers would show up with the most impressive press jobs. It had an effect.

Not a shift went by when I didn't hear a favorable remark about my uniform. When a server approaches looking sharp, crisp and well-groomed, the guest is more likely to tip for that level of professionalism.

15% Tip: The least you should do is take a shower and have a clean uniform.

20% Tip: The sharper your appearance, the more your employer will notice and reward you with better shifts.

30% Tip: Take extra time to starch your uniform and tighten your look. You may be amazed that by doing this one thing, your tips will increase dramatically.

What's *your* style?

YOUR APPROACH TELLS SO MUCH

Up to this point in the sequence of service, we have yet to come in contact with our guests. But now, it is finally showtime! The time has come to put all of this learning together and engage the guest.

Your approach begins before you make a move. If you are visible to the guest, they may be 'reading' you, the same as you are 'reading' them. Are you gossiping? Slouching? Are you judging them in a way that they notice, by making remarks to other servers?

In many restaurants these days, you will find huddles of servers in the corners chatting, gossiping, and goofing around while they wait for guests to be seated in their respective sections. Your guests are watching.

Here is the bottom line: *Are your guests important to you?*

Every move you make should reflect the importance of each and every guest. It will be noticeable in everything you do, from the way you respond to questions to how you walk to and from their table.

As you begin your walk to the table, your pace should be quick to let them know they are your priority. How many times have you been in a restaurant and wondered if your server knew you were there? Or when they did know, they took their time, perhaps engaging in a conversation with a fellow employee en route. Not a good feeling – when you're the guest. Also, now is the time to engage in eye contact, even though you are not quite yet at the table. Smile as you approach. Let your guests know by your movements and expressions that you are glad they are there.

Hustle to and from the table. The guest should get the feeling that your number one job is to serve them (which, of course, it is). You also stand out like a sore thumb when you are the only server doing it. When I worked at a farm-to-table restaurant in Tennessee, I moved quickly when delivering items to my guests. Curiously, new servers often asked, "What's your hurry? You only have *one* table."

My typical response was a smile. Sometimes it's nice - and lucrative - to stand out from the crowd.

15% Tip: Smile genuinely at your guests as you walk toward them. *They* are your priority.

20% Tip: Go easy at first with your greeting. Try not to frighten the guests during your initial approach.

30% Tip: Moving quickly lets guests know how important they are. Moving *too* quickly lets them know you're a weirdo.

What's *your* style?

READING AND GREETING THE GUESTS

Have you read the book *The Face Reader*, by Patrician McCarthy? The basic premise is that there are certain facial structures (and even wrinkles!) that can reveal different parts of your personality.

For example, the book ascertains that if you have vertical wrinkles in front of your earlobes, you are a natural bullshit detector. Whether or not you believe that, there are interesting insights in this book that are helpful when serving guests.

'Reading' the guest comes with experience, but some aspects of reading people come from basic common sense. When you approach your table for the first time, you have the opportunity to gain valuable information as you study your guests' faces, body language, conversation level, and clothing. Yes, you are making a judgment. You are, in a sense, classifying your guests and making assumptions.

For example, as your guests take their seats, you notice that no one is talking. They sit in an orderly fashion, not smiling, but are dressed nicely and well groomed. Some fidget with the flatware. Others immediately begin looking at the menu. Do you greet with, "Hey, everyone! Why the sour faces?? Did you just come from a funeral?" Probably not.

This example of a poor greeting reminds me of a funny story. On a typically slammed Friday night at a packed restaurant, I approached a party of eight to greet them. I raised my voice above the fray, almost yelling, "Good evening! First, allow me to apologize for the noise level in here!"

As I was speaking, a young lady from the group began to 'sign' what I had said. Each person at the table smiled as though the joke were on me. It was. They were all deaf and I was apologizing for the noise. Brilliant!

So what's the lesson? Ease into your greeting. Although you will gain an initial read as you approach, you will continue to understand your guests more and more with each visit. Take your time. Say hello and wait for a reaction. This alone can tell you a great deal about how you will adjust your service as you go. If I had waited for a reaction in the above scenario, I likely would've known this table of guests was deaf. And I wouldn't have made the comment I did.

15% Tip: Avoid rushing the guests. If you are unable to spend an appropriate amount of time during your introduction, let them know you will be right back.

20% Tip: Your greeting will set the tone, so take charge and know what you are going to say before you reach the table.

30% Tip: During the greeting, you and your guests are feeling each other out, much like boxers in a ring. Don't throw your big punches too early.

What's *your* style?

AT THE TABLE

When I was 18, I was going to school in Oklahoma while working at a swanky Chinese restaurant called Mandarin Garden. I was a back waiter (or glorified busboy), and I learned a great deal about presentation and plate handling from this cool server named Joel.

Joel was a bit older than me, and I was especially impressed with the way he carried himself. His posture was perfect, his walk confident and he said no more than he had to at the table. We all wanted to be like him. He was a consummate technical professional. Joel relied on his style and class to make his money. He knew the menu as well as the chef, and he could recommend and upsell better than anybody. But his forte was his plates.

As Joel's busboy, I had a front row seat to learn his techniques. Before each course, Joel strutted to the table in a calculated rhythm, stopped, turned, and crisply snapped a clean towel from his arm. With military-like precision, Joel retrieved a plate from the stack, and made a spectacle of wiping the plate. Then, with quick cat-like movements, smartly whipped a plate in front of each guest, from their left, ladies first.

Joel's presentation was impressive. Guests returned to the restaurant because of his serving style.

Your presence at the table, your posture and level of comfort are all evaluated (consciously or not) by the guests. Stand upright. Never slouch or lean on the table.

Some places encourage sitting with guests, but I don't recommend that practice. If your guests are your friends, they might invite you to join them. But sitting with your guests is not your decision to make. There is an invisible barrier that is best not to cross, unless the guest openly invites it. Even then, crossing that barrier can be a disservice to your guests.

On the other hand, some of the greatest joys that servers experience is when genuine rapport develops with their guests.

While serving an outgoing couple on their anniversary one night in Tennessee, I began to feel the connection that servers often experience with special guests.

Subtle to start, our rapport began to gain steam as the night rolled on. It seemed that everything I said was hilarious to them.

As I was opening a bottle of wine, the gentleman noticed a bandage on my index finger, and he asked about it. I brushed it off as no big deal, identifying my captain's knife as the culprit. He took the opportunity to show me a small cut on his knuckle that he had sustained at work that day. The contest was on.

I rolled up my sleeve to reveal a miniscule scar on my inside elbow. He immediately pulled up his pant leg to display his own invisible battle wound from years before. The wife was getting such a kick out of our silliness that I thought it appropriate - although maybe not for most parties - to go for the big one.

I pulled up my apron, and said, "Well, that's got nothing on my vasectomy scar..."

"NO!!!" the woman hollered, with a beaming smile on her face. We all burst out laughing. They tipped me 40% that night.

15% Tip: You are constantly judged and evaluated by your guests. Learn to see yourself with their eyes.

20% Tip: Don't come off too strong, too early. Ease into your relationship with guests. Let them recognize and enjoy your personal style without shoving it down their throat.

30% Tip: Building true rapport with your guests can have a major impact on your income.

What's *your* style?

HOW TO SERVE FOOD AND DRINK

One of the finer things in life is being served in a professional manner.

When a server swoops in to clear a plate or deliver one with a certain sense of style and polish, it is impressive.

Following are basic rules of service that you may already know, but are worth a review.

When delivering plates, serve guests from their left whenever possible, with your left hand, ladies first.

Keep thumbs and fingers off the plate, utilizing only the rim of the plate.

Serve beverages by holding the glass at the base or stem and delivering to the guest's right-hand side.

Flatware is placed by holding the sides of the base, placing knives and spoons to the right with your right hand, and placing forks to the left with your left hand.

Coffee cups are placed to the right (unless you notice the guest is left-handed), with the handle at three or four o'clock.

As you deliver a plate of any kind (appetizer, salad, dinner, dessert), slide it in front of the guest, and announce, for example, "Your blue cheese salad, sir." You don't want to be the server who says, "Okay, who had the steak well done?" Avoiding this all-too-common mistake of 'auctioning' items requires that you know your position or seat numbers (as well as your food!).

One of my own personal guidelines regarding service is to do the *most* to make myself look like *less* of a fool. If I know exactly who had what, I won't look like a total goof by asking.

Move around the table effortlessly. This may take some practice. For me, it was almost like a dance step as I placed a plate and then moved to the next guest. This movement should appear smooth, confident and professional.

Keep your body and face as far from the food as you can as you deliver.

Do your best not to use your inside arm to deliver items. In other words, try to keep your body open so you don't elbow the guest in the mouth.

Once all plates have been placed, it is important to make sure your guests have all they need before you leave them. The server who makes consistent cash thinks of these considerations beforehand and anticipates the needs of their guests.

For example, you've delivered two guests their entrées. One ordered a steak, medium rare with a baked potato. The other, lobster tail with steamed vegetables. A salad course preceded the entrées. Before the entrées came out, you meticulously prepared the table for the next course: removed all the salad plates, replaced any used silverware (as needed), and refilled beverages. For the steak, you delivered a steak knife (and possibly steak sauce and lobster butter, depending on the restaurant) to the table *before* the entrées arrived.

WINE SERVICE

Your level of comfort is probably the most important aspect when it comes to wine service. You should feel completely at ease and confident, which can only be achieved with practice.

When you approach the host (the one who ordered the wine), hold the bottle at the base, with the label facing the guest at eye level. I like to cup the bottle with a napkin underneath. You then say the name and vintage of the wine, and wait for the guest to respond (hopefully, in the affirmative). Once approved, you begin the opening process. Many servers utilize a 'captain's knife' style wine opener (my choice, as well), but you will need to choose what works best for you and your restaurant.

Some establishments allow you to place the bottle on the table as you open. In the case where you must keep it in your hands, it becomes a bit trickier, but still easily done with practice.

Either way, figure out the most comfortable approach, and begin by cutting the cover around the bottom ridge of the lip with the blade on your captain's knife. Remove the cut portion of the cover and place it in your pocket. Pull the corkscrew out of the captain's knife and situate the point into the center of the cork, turning your knife clockwise.

Once you have buried the corkscrew, anchor your knife against the lip with the metal lever and pull up to extract the cork. With your napkin, gently pull the cork from the bottle the rest of the way and present it to the host. Do so silently. Making a loud 'pop' is a rookie mistake.

Take your napkin and gently wipe any cork from the lip and then pour a small taste (about an ounce) into the host's glass for approval. Ensure that the label is facing the guest as you pour. If they like it, begin with ladies at the table (elders first, if possible), pouring about three to four ounces each. Then finish with the gentlemen, and finally the host. Always make sure there is enough left in the bottle for the host!

More information on how to serve food and drink will be discussed in the next section, Sequence of Service (SOS).

15% Tip: Practice silent service. The guest doesn't always want to hear you open your mouth every time you approach. You can refill beverages, remove plates, replace flatware, etc., without saying a word.

20% Tip: Know your position numbers so that you may deliver an item without asking the guest a thing. Instead, with confidence, announce the dish and place it in front of the guest, from the left, ladies first.

30% Tip: When the guest needs to ask you for nothing, you have succeeded.

What's *your* style?

THE SEQUENCE OF SERVICE

Most places will have a training program, which addresses something I call The Sequence of Service (SOS). This is the order in which events should happen at any given table of guests.

When you are managing multiple tables, the SOS can keep you focused and on point regarding where each table is in the sequence. Obviously, depending on the guests, you will not be able to hit every single point, every single time, at every single table. Many guests will have a time schedule, know what they want when they arrive, or might not want to hear you talk about the menu (or anything else). That is why reading your guests is of utmost importance.

GREET THE TABLE WITHIN ONE MINUTE – When your guests are seated, get yourself over there pronto! If you are at another table, delivering food or beverages, try to get your new table's attention to let them know you see them and will be right over - while remaining focused on your current table. You are reading your new guests, and they are reading you. How important are they to you? Let them know from the beginning.

HAVE THEY BEEN HERE BEFORE? This factor is especially important when determining how much time you will need to spend with your guests during the introduction. If they are new to your establishment, they will not be familiar with the menu. The good server takes the time to guide them through the menu, offering recommendations.

At Bobby McGee's, we were taught that this step should be treated as though you are their tour guide, guiding them through the selections. This is an effective way to go about your introduction because it places you in the socks of the guest.

ABOUT THE MENU - Since you are talking with the guests for the first time in the Sequence of Service, it is important not to come on too strong. As I mentioned earlier, you want to ease into your introduction. The same goes for making your first sale.

Many servers will not make any suggestions and wait for the guest to decide what to do about a beverage or starter. That's not style, that's *laziness*. Find a selling approach that works with your personality. For me, it usually came with a hint of humor, but you have to understand your guests and watch yourself so that you don't go overboard.

When I was serving at a country club near Denver, I tried my humor on some sweet older ladies while describing the featured items at lunch. Painting a picture, I told of the tuna on grilled rye, the Rueben on rye and the delicious French onion soup with rye croutons. In conclusion, I said with a smile and a wink, "I think we're trying to move the rye."

Moments later, my manager pulled me aside to let me know that the ladies had called him over and wondered why we were serving stale bread. I didn't see that one coming. Like I said before, go easy at first.

SELL SOMETHING BEFORE YOU LEAVE

Once you have finished guiding your guests through the menu and offering suggestions, you need to have a decision from them before you leave. Are they having a drink from the bar, or perhaps non-alcoholic beverages? What about an appetizer? These are all decisions you need to know before you leave the table for the first time.

My style is easygoing, but certainly not laid back. My posture is upright and professional, and I engage by eye contact and by listening.

When establishing eye contact, I find it effective to slightly lean toward the person as you are engaging, but obviously, not in a creeper type of way.

It seems simple, but not everyone has mastery of it. Truly listening and truly *hearing* a guest can make a significant difference in your income. The easiest way to listen is to *not talk*.

One behavior that absolutely drives me nuts is when a server utters a canned response as the guest talks, confirming that the server is indeed not listening. This quick "Yeah, yeah," or "Uh huh," followed by an interruption is all too common.

Stop and actively listen. Not only will this be a refreshing change for the guest, it will also save you valuable time by truly understanding what your guest wants. A trick to doing this is to parrot back the order. I have seen many servers struggle with repeating back at first, often sounding like little robots or recording devices.

Here's how it might sound when done well. A couple is seated in your section and upon delivering your introduction and suggesting some beverages, they decide on a couple of drinks from the bar:

Guest: "My wife would like a vodka martini with olives...and I want a Bud draft."

You: "Yes...so many vodkas to choose from. Stoli? Perhaps Ketel One? (Notice I offered two upsale choices and repeated the order.)

Guest: "Oh, she likes Ketel."

You: "Ketel...very wise! Up? And maybe dirty??" (Because she likes olives, I offer 'dirty.' My general assumption with martinis is that most people like them served 'up.' If not, they will correct me).

Guest: " Perfect!"

You: "And for you, sir, the 16-ounce bud or the big boy? 24 ounces?"

Guest: "The big boy."

You: "That's what I'm talkin' about! I will be back with your dirty Ketel martini and your Big Bud...please take your time looking over our menu, and I look forward to answering your questions when I get back."

RING ORDER IN POS (point of sale system)

The old days of handwritten tickets are gone unless you work in certain diners or truck stops. There are a few older restaurants that still utilize this system, but it is likely you will work, or are working, in a place that has a computerized system. Once you receive an order of any kind from your guests, immediately ring it into the POS.

Knowing your POS can be almost as important as knowing your menu. This is where you will lose speed and efficiency if you are not proficient. Take the time to get to know where everything is, from all menu items to add-ons, substitutions, credit card payments, split payments, etc. Managers worth their sea salt will gladly allow a server extra time during off-hours to practice on the POS. Take advantage of it. When your fingers fly on the monitor without thinking, your service excellence will increase. Confidence. Speed. Style.

You will save yourself, the restaurant, and your guests a great deal of aggravation if you take the time to carefully review your order before you push Send. All too often, servers are in such a rush that they forget to review, sending a wrong order to the kitchen. This error will ultimately result in remaking an item and costing the restaurant more money. It will also delay the sequence of service for that table, throwing the timing off. Ten seconds reviewing the order prevents a lot of trouble and missteps – and prevents a lesser tip for you.

PREPARE THE TABLE – Every time you ring an item into the system, identify precisely what should be at the table before that item arrives. At this point of the SOS, one of the most common items will be an appetizer.

Let's say you ring in an order of fried clams for a party of four. Immediately after you send this through the POS, what do you think you should have on the table beforehand? If you answered, "Some kind of plates and perhaps a serving spoon," you are a genius!

As always, deliver it before they need it. If you make it a habit to complete this step immediately after you ring into the POS, you will constantly be a step ahead.

DELIVER ITEMS

When delivering beverages, always hold the glass at the bottom, avoiding the rim completely. Wine glasses should be held by the stem at the base. The most important factors are stability and cleanliness. Keep your fingers off the rims. As you place, it is customary to put the glass in front of the guest's right-hand side.

When using a tray with beverages, make sure you are balanced before removing a beverage. I have seen servers drop trays and spill on guests because they didn't realize this rule of physics. If you are new, this may take some practice. So, practice.

At the Melting Pot, our dining room had three distinct levels spanning three separate floors with an open drop in the middle. It goes without saying that the servers had to be in decent shape to climb the flights of stairs from the kitchen on the bottom floor, to the bar on the third floor.

One night, one of my new servers was carrying two white Russians from the bar on his tray. As he reached the top of the stairs, he lost control of the tray, and the drinks (in slow-motion style) flew down two flights of stairs and crashed on a table below, shattering and splashing vodka, Kahlua and cream all over the guests. From then on, that server (who became a favorite of mine) was known only as 'Drago.' (For fans of the *Rocky* series, you'll remember Drago was the name of the white Russian played by Dolph Lundgren in *Rocky III*).

Some restaurants will have large tray service for hot items and others will have you carry plates on your arms and hands. Both styles require repetition to be comfortable.

When carrying plates on a large tray, balance is the key. These trays are heavy and awkward, so it is important to bend your knees when picking up and dropping off, as well as maintain a balanced base with your body. Tricky at first, you will find that once you are comfortable, your grace and style will be easily reflected in how you handle a large serving tray.

If you are required to carry plates by hand, my general rule of thumb is to keep your thumb and fingers off the rim of the plate.

While it is impressive for a server to balance four or five plates on his arms, I prefer three. When you have too many, it becomes extremely cumbersome to properly place the item in front of the guest. You will often look like a balancing act on a high-wire at the circus. As discussed earlier, your delivery should be smooth and seamless. Doing so requires space and use of your arms and hands.

CHECK BACK

I used to serve at a swanky place in downtown Denver called The Trinity Grill. The owner's philosophy was that the food was so good that we didn't have to ask the guest if it was prepared to their liking. There is certainly an air of confidence to this way of thinking. However, it is my opinion that the guest enjoys being checked on.

Often, there will be something the guest may need regardless of how well you prepared the table. As far as steaks are concerned, many restaurants will ask the guest to cut into it upon delivery to ensure proper temperature.

When it comes to checking back, be creative and inventive. Asking "How is everything?" is a complete cop-out. Don't allow yourself to get in the habit of sounding robotic or canned. Instead, challenge yourself to extend your vocabulary.

One of my greatest pet peeves is the trite response, "No problem." This phrase seems to be common nowadays, and is too often used to communicate, "You're welcome." I personally don't think the word 'problem' should be part of your verbiage. It automatically conjures up feelings of negativity. The guest might be thinking, "Am I bothering you by being here?" Is serving a guest typically a 'problem?' Develop a different response. When a guest says, "Thank you," a professional response is, "My pleasure," or something to that effect.

I was recently at an Arby's drive-through, ordering my usual roast beef sandwich. When the pleasant young lady gave me the total and asked me to drive forward, I gave my typical thoughtful and courteous reply of, "Thank you!" Through the small mounted speaker came a surprising reply, "Oh, yes, sir! I am happy to help!"

What?? You are *happy* to help? Who says that?

You can imagine my surprise upon hearing her comment. Reaching the delivery window, I told the nice girl how great I thought her reply was and asked her if she came up with that wonderful response. She candidly told me that it was a corporate directive, that everyone is required to respond in kind and that it had become an inside joke to the employees. That's a shame, because I really liked the verbiage.

REMOVE ITEMS / PREPARE TABLE

One of my least favorite ways of determining whether a guest is finished is by asking, "Are you still working on that?" Dining isn't work. A better way is by reading the guest. If they have pushed the plate away, placed all their flatware or napkin on the plate, they are likely done. If you are unsure, ask if you may take their plate. When you do, remove it from the guest's right-hand side whenever possible. Once all unneeded items are removed, return to clean and prepare the table for the next course.

DESSERT PRESENTATION

Once the guests are finished with the main course, completely clear the table, leaving only the beverages. Wipe or 'crumb' the table if necessary before presenting the desserts. A favorite tactic of mine is to never ask about dessert, but show up with the dessert tray once everything has been cleared. (A dessert tray is a display of fresh desserts for the guests to view.)

It's fun to see the expressions and body language of the guests as I approach with desserts; the waving of the hands, the exasperated looks indicating, *"No way!"* As they begin to look at the dessert display, I say something like, "Just thought I would check...," and I wait for a response. As with any other course, prepare the table with the proper flatware and sharing plates, etc.

CHECK PRESENTATION

Once the guests have finished and the table is cleared (or in some cases, during the dessert course), it is time to present the guest check. It is rare when you know ahead of time who will be paying, so place the check in a neutral location. Let them know that you enjoyed serving them, thank them graciously, and invite them back. You should also communicate that you will be back when they are ready to take care of the payment.

When picking up a cash payment, stay away from the common phrase, "Do you need change?" This unprofessional statement implies that whatever is left over must be the tip. Servers who use this verbiage are obviously not concerned about the guest, but themselves. A better way to collect a payment is to say, "I will be right back with your change." If the change is yours, the guest will let you know.

15% Tip: Know where each table is in the sequence. This will keep you organized and on point.

20% Tip: The quicker and more concise your introduction, the better. There is a fine balance to getting in and getting out quickly without making the guests feel rushed. To accomplish this feat, your style and communication needs to be smooth.

30% Tip: The top server commands multiple tables at once. The only way to execute this feat with excellence at each table is to have a mastery of the SOS. This excellence is all-encompassing, from complete food and beverage knowledge to mastery of the point of sale system.

What's *your* style?

TEAMWORK, HUSTLE, ATTITUDE

Making more money isn't only about your knowledge and style but also about your work ethic. Not only will your guest notice the hustle and teamwork, but your employer will, as well. If you are looking to get promoted in this business, there is no better way than to possess these traits. On the flip side, it is obvious to an employer which employees show these traits to kiss up to the boss, and those who genuinely demonstrate them for the benefit of the guests.

Believe it or not, a guest will tip you on your performance at other tables as well as their own. Maybe you have experienced it. Your server has been exceptional at your table, exceeding your expectations, doing everything right. What makes it even more impressive is that they are hustling throughout the dining room, delivering food at other servers' tables with the same enthusiasm and professionalism they showed you. They smile, open doors, pull out chairs and are clearly enjoying their job. A savvy guest will generally reward such genuine behavior.

As with any industry, there will be those who do not have this same work ethic. They won't run any other server's food but their own, and they can usually be found sitting down in the back or smoking a cigarette somewhere. We have all seen them and realize what a drain they can be to the rest of us servers. Often, you are covering their butts by taking care of their guests.

Regarding attitude, as general manager of the Melting Pot, I established the restaurant as a 'no gripe zone.' Any and all complaints were to be addressed with the manager at the end of the shift. In other words, if you're going to moan and groan about something, 'game time' is not the appropriate time.

Unfortunately, it is common to have what I call 'poison pills' on your staff. These are the folks who will complain about anything and everything. Not surprisingly, they are also the ones who make the smallest tips. Go figure. Stay away from these vultures because they will suck the joy out of your work environment. Instead, be that server whose great attitude is contagious.

I have often related serving guests to acting on stage. Even when you don't feel like it, the show must go on. Sometimes you need to put on your game face and perform - if you want to make money, that is.

15% Tip: When you walk through the doors to your restaurant, your attitude should reflect a heart for service.

20% Tip: Set a quick pace that you are able to keep throughout your shift. This is the speed at which you will move through the restaurant.

30% Tip: Have you been to a place where there is that one server who seems to be thoroughly enjoying the job, floating through the dining room effortlessly, joking and having fun? We see them at other tables, can hear the enthusiasm in their voice and wish they were *our* server. That's you. *You* are that server.

What's *your* style?

SALESMANSHIP

As the GM of the Melting Pot, it was my responsibility to develop a server training program similar to what you read here. Like any other training or teaching method, it is only as good as the effort put in by the individual server.

One of my favorite servers was a smart young man named Trevor. He had been working on his master's degree (he is now a teacher, and an excellent one!), and served to make his money to pay for college.

We sold a lot of wine, and Trevor didn't know much about wine when he started serving with us. But he was smart enough to realize that the higher the check, the more money he would make on the percentage. Simple math.

The consummate student, he took it upon himself to learn wine by studying books and participating in wine classes. His sales soared through the roof and he quickly became one of the top earning servers. Other servers would often approach him with their questions. Not only did his checks go up, his requests did, too.

Guests enjoy being taken care of by a server who knows what to recommend and why. On top of this, Trevor got the best shifts because any managers in their right minds will schedule their top sellers on the busiest nights. Duh.

As with any profession or job, what you put in is what you get out. The money is there for a server who is a 'student of the game.'

Speaking of games, a quick note about 'suggestive selling:' Guests are aware of this game that has been going on for years. The server says something like, "Would you care for an order of chicken wings, or would you prefer our fried mushrooms to start?"

"Well, genius, I don't want either one. How 'bout that?"

Perhaps a better approach would be to give a couple of recommendations and then leave them alone to look things over. The exceptional server is one who knows the menu well enough to paint a verbal picture of the item, leaving the guest no choice but to try it.

15% Tip: The best way to know your menu is to try the items. The guest usually wants to know what you like and recommend.

20% Tip: The more genuine you are, the more the guest will respond.

30% Tip: If the opportunity exists within your establishment, cross train in the kitchen and behind the bar. You will be amazed at what you learn.

What's *your* style?

GIVE YOURSELF A RAISE

Here is a list of some of the simple things (some little, some big) that will separate you from the rest of the servers and showcase your personal serving style.

EXCEEDING EXPECTATIONS

We have already discussed certain ways in which to exceed guest expectations. Anticipating their needs - getting them what they want before they realize they want it - is the main ingredient for exceeding expectations. This skill requires an acute awareness of precisely what's going on at the table.

For example, all the guests at your table are heartily enjoying their food - but one. That individual is picking at the food, perhaps looking at it with disappointment. The excellent server will take notice and tactfully inquire about the dish. At this point in the SOS, you have already established your style with the guests.

Personally, I would approach that guest quietly, lean in and say something like, "Not doin' it for ya, is it?" When they respond in the affirmative, I immediately remove the dish and present a menu, so they can select something else. "Here's the menu, unless you already know what you would like...?"

Many poor servers will roll their eyes, grab the dish and stomp off in a huff if a guest is unhappy with a selection. The stellar server will act swiftly, communicate the new order to the kitchen, and make the guest comfortable, by taking care of the situation cheerfully.

OPENING DOORS

As guests leave your section, hustle to the door to open it for them, thank them and say goodbye.

CHASING AFTER GUESTS

Make it a rule not to inspect your tip in view of the guests. When a generous tip is received, it is important to thank that guest. Sometimes I have chased guests to the parking lot (or an adjacent store) to say, "Thank you!"

RETRIEVE A VALET TICKET OR COAT CHECK

Some establishments offer valet parking or coat check services. The good server will ask the guests, if, as their server, they might retrieve the guests' ticket(s) for them as they leave.

This reminds me of a funny story. I was a manager at a high-end restaurant in downtown Denver. Guests could park in the skyrise parking lot attached to our building, but needed their ticket validated so they didn't have to pay the parking fee. Often, guests would approach me at the host stand to get their ticket stamped, or validated. One time, a sharply dressed gentleman approached me following his lunch and asked, "Can you validate me, please?" Without skipping a beat, I said, "Well, yes I can! Let me say that you have selected the perfect tie for that suit, and you are a striking man with purpose to his step!" He paused, looked at me for a brief second with a puzzled look on his face, and then we both laughed and laughed.

ESCORTING TO THE RESTROOM

One of the many small things you can do is to walk a guest to the restroom. When asked where the restrooms are, instead of pointing, say something like, "Follow me," and subtly walk toward the restroom area until it's in view. Taking a few extra seconds for this kind of gesture will separate you from other servers. (However, the restroom door is one you won't be opening for the guest. That's weird. Don't be weird.)

PLACING NAPKIN ON LAP

For many fine dining establishments, it is customary to pick up the napkin from the table and lay it gently on the laps of guests, with their permission. Not everyone will want you to do this. If you are in fine dining, your restaurant will have specific rules for this. If it is part of procedure, my approach is simply to touch the napkin as I push in their chair and ask, "May I?"

PULLING OUT CHAIRS

When you are at your table when your guests arrive, it is such a nice - and easy - touch to pull out chairs for the ladies. Another easy gesture is to be there when a guest returns from the restroom to pull out a chair. Cha ching. You just made more money.

ALWAYS GIVE WAY

The guest is always the priority. Many times, you will be rushing through the dining room as a guest is walking through. Whether or not your hands are full, stop and let the guest pass. How important are they to you? Let them know, whether or not the guest is from your table.

KNOWLEDGE AND UPSELLING

When talking about the food, paint a verbal picture of the item. Tell the guest what you personally enjoy about it and why. If you are an expert on the menu, you will easily lead the service staff in sales. *Easily.*

BE EARLY

Managers spend a great deal of time creating a schedule. When a server is late, panic sets in. Are you a server who can be depended on to show up on time, every time?

WORK ETHIC

Having a great work ethic can be seen through hustle, properly completing side-work, teamwork, staying late, cross-training, and covering your shifts instead of calling in absent.

THE GUEST IS ALWAYS RIGHT, RIGHT?

The short answer is no. The guest is not always right. However, your reaction to a challenging guest can always be right.

When I was a manager in Cherry Creek, I noticed a guy at one of the tables acting strange, almost drunk. As I approached, I realized he was most definitely drunk, loud and pretty obnoxious. I kindly escorted him out.

Was the guest right?

Of course not.

Was I right to have him leave?

Absolutely.

Was it strange that the same guy delivered a pizza to my house that night?

Priceless.

Here's the thing. Don't get into an argument with a guest or become combative. Some guests are miserable and will never be pleased. Always get a manager involved when you begin to see the signs of a disgruntled guest.

A WORD ABOUT GRATITUDE

As someone who works for tips, it is often easy to take it personally when someone dogs you in the gratuity. Don't take it personally! There is always the uncontrollable factor of the guests themselves. You never know what's going on in their lives.

You've heard, no doubt, the saying, "Don't judge someone unless you have walked a mile in their shoes." Sometimes it is difficult to place yourself there, especially when you are relying on tips to pay the rent. But do your best to give the benefit of the doubt.

The good news is that bad tipping is generally rare when you are an excellent server. Sure, you will have those nights when nothing seems to be going right. (Is there a full moon??) But the important thing is to view in it the long-term.

So many servers will walk into a shift, and say something like, "Man, I got to make a hundred tonight to make rent!" Try not to put so much pressure on a shift. Get on a budget to manage your cash. That way, it will be easier to swallow when, as an outstanding server, you get that rare bad tip.

Many guests are on a tight budget, and often save for months for that big night out. If you are genuinely interested in the needs of the guests, you will be naturally empathetic when your tip is not what you expect. Don't worry, it all works out in the long run. In the meantime, bitching about your tips will categorize you as someone not really fit for this business.

BEHIND THE SCENES

Unfortunately, I have worked at several restaurants where the front of the house always seems to be at war with the back of the house. In many restaurant cultures, chefs have little respect for servers, and often think of servers as whining complainers. Much of the time they are right.

Look at it from the chef's perspective. Many servers will not take the time to learn the menu, relying solely on their 'wonderful' personality to carry the day. During the most inopportune times (the line is slammed with 30 tickets hanging in the window), an unprepared server is likely to interrupt to ask about the ingredients in a certain menu item, or something along those lines. Learn the menu. Know the answer. When you do, you will become the cook's best friend, and that's a good thing to be.

WHAT ARE YOU WAITING FOR?

Why do you serve others? Are you motivated by money, or does it go a little deeper than that? For more than 25 years, I have watched servers, trained them, mentored them, and learned from them. One common denominator in all those years has been this: The servers who genuinely enjoy taking care of other people, and know their menu, will ultimately make the most money.

Conversely, servers who care only about how much they will get tipped ultimately make the least money, and don't survive for long in the business. (And if they do, you avoid them and their establishment like the plague!)

The hospitality industry is in desperate need of people like you! You have a genuine desire to treat others with kindness. Your smile is warm and engaging, your personality the same. You have a tremendous work ethic and have the passion and desire to perfect your craft through knowledge and practice – or you wouldn't have read this book. You are that super server!

So, what's *your* style, how will you and your guests benefit from it - and what are you *Waiting* for?

www.ingramcontent.com/pod-product-compliance
Lightning Source LLC
Chambersburg PA
CBHW051406250726
48656CB00006B/2297